ON EARTH

written and illustrated by

G. BRIAN KARAS

G. P. PUTNAM'S SONS   NEW YORK

G. P. PUTNAM'S SONS

A division of Penguin Young Readers Group

Published by The Penguin Group

Penguin Group (USA) Inc., 375 Hudson Street, New York, NY 10014, U.S.A.

Penguin Group (Canada), 10 Alcorn Avenue, Toronto, Ontario, Canada M4V 3B2 (a division of Pearson Penguin Canada Inc.)

Penguin Books Ltd, 80 Strand, London WC2R 0RL, England.

Penguin Ireland, 25 St. Stephen's Green, Dublin 2, Ireland (a division of Penguin Books Ltd.)

Penguin Books India Pvt Ltd, 11 Community Centre, Panchsheel Park, New Delhi - 110 017, India.

Penguin Group (NZ), Cnr Airborne and Rosedale Roads, Albany, Auckland, New Zealand (a division of Pearson New Zealand Ltd).

Penguin Books (South Africa) (Pty) Ltd, 24 Sturdee Avenue, Rosebank, Johannesburg 2196, South Africa.

Penguin Books Ltd, Registered Offices: 80 Strand, London WC2R 0RL, England.

Published simultaneously in Canada. Manufactured in China by South China Printing Co. Ltd.

Design by Gina DiMassi. Text set in Woodland Demi.

Library of Congress Cataloging-in-Publication Data

Karas, G. Brian.

On Earth / G. Brian Karas.

p. cm.   1. Earth—Juvenile literature. I. Title.

QB631.4.K37 2005   525—dc22   2004018204

ISBN 0-399-24025-X

10 9 8 7 6 5 4 3 2 1

First Impression

For Brooke and Rick

with special thanks to Carl Mayer

On earth
we go for a giant ride in space,
spinning like a merry-go-round.

The earth spins on its axis

AXIS

REVOLUTION

ROTATION

and circles the sun in a great sweep.

We face the sun,
    its light and warmth,
        as we live our days.

Shadows get long
as day rolls into night.

At night we turn away from the sun
and see a universe of stars and planets

while we dream of
what we can do tomorrow.

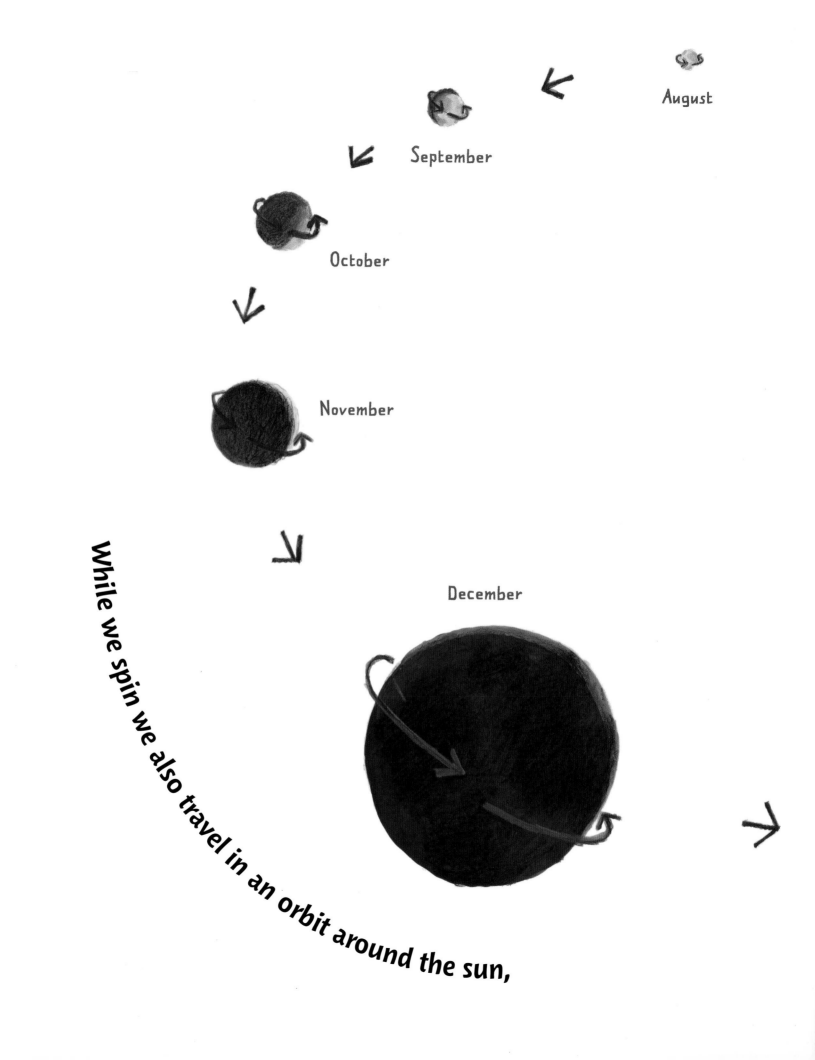

August

September

October

November

December

While we spin we also travel in an orbit around the sun,

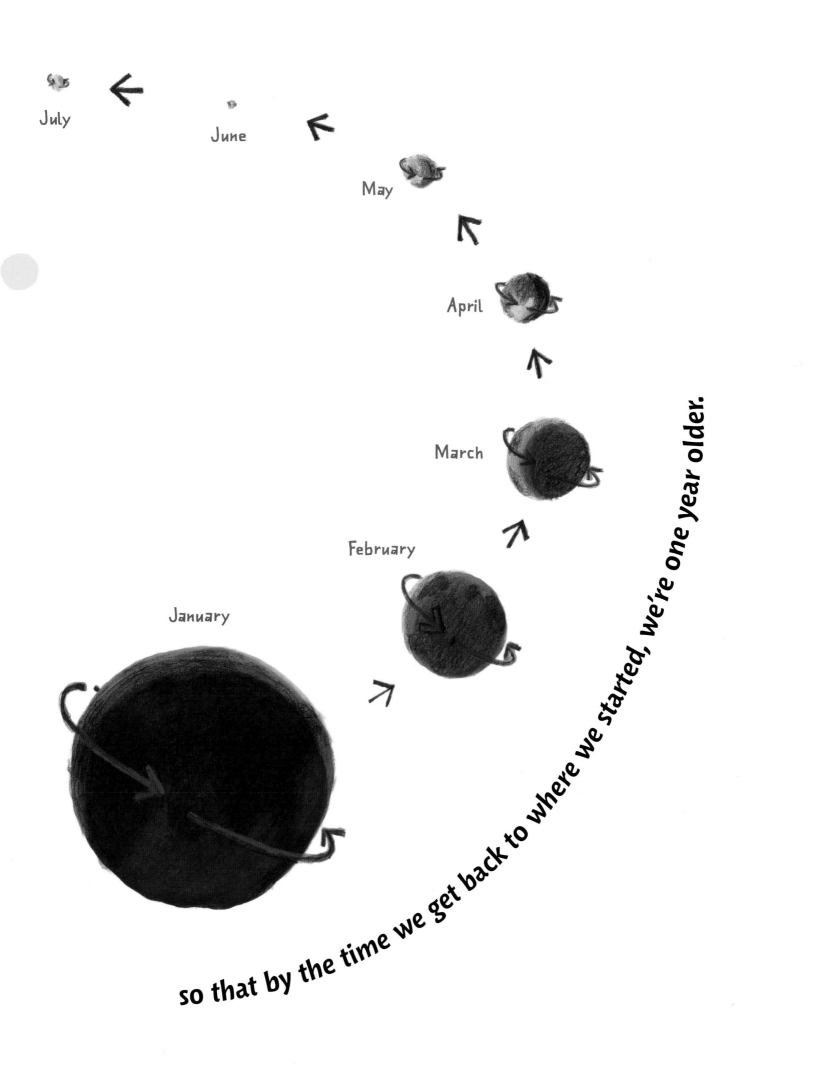

July

June

May

April

March

February

January

so that by the time we get back to where we started, we're one year older.

We count months as we grow.

In twelve months a year has gone by.

Years go by,
day by day.
We count them with
calendars and candles.

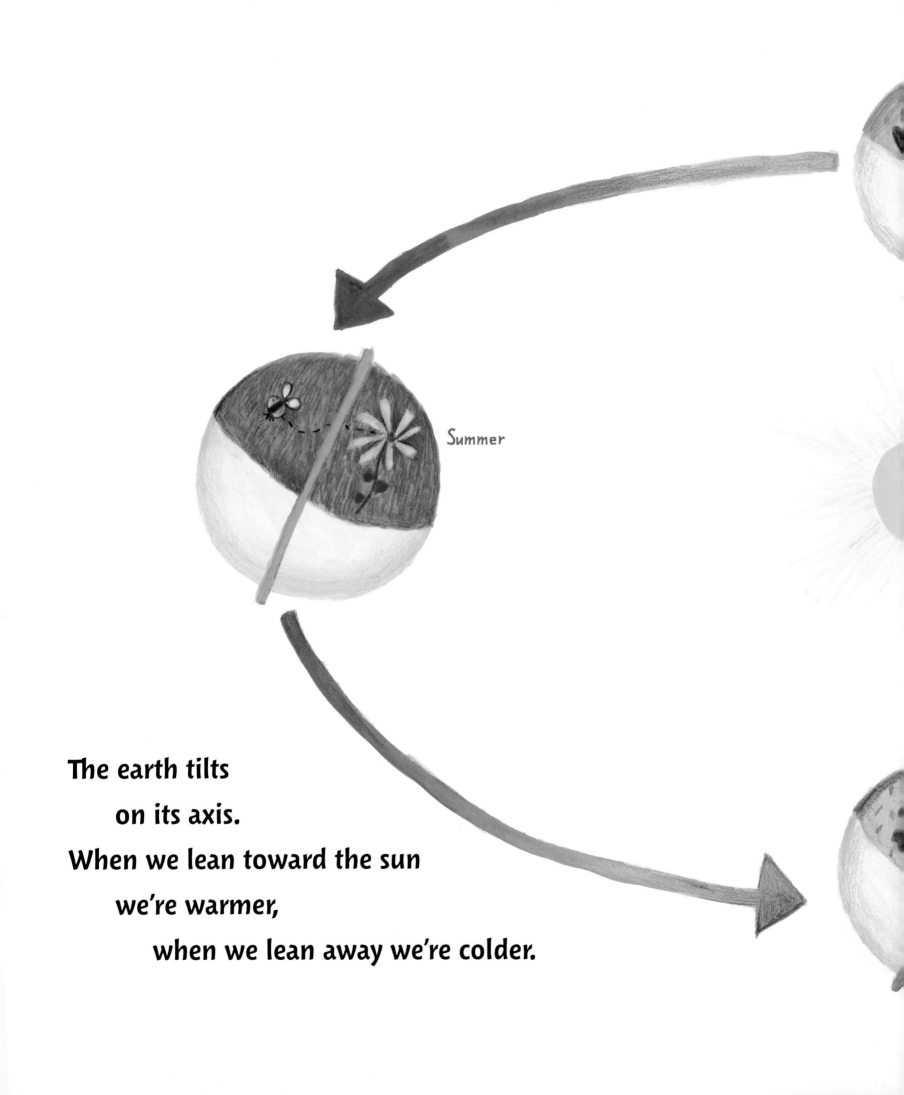

Summer

The earth tilts
    on its axis.
When we lean toward the sun
    we're warmer,
        when we lean away we're colder.

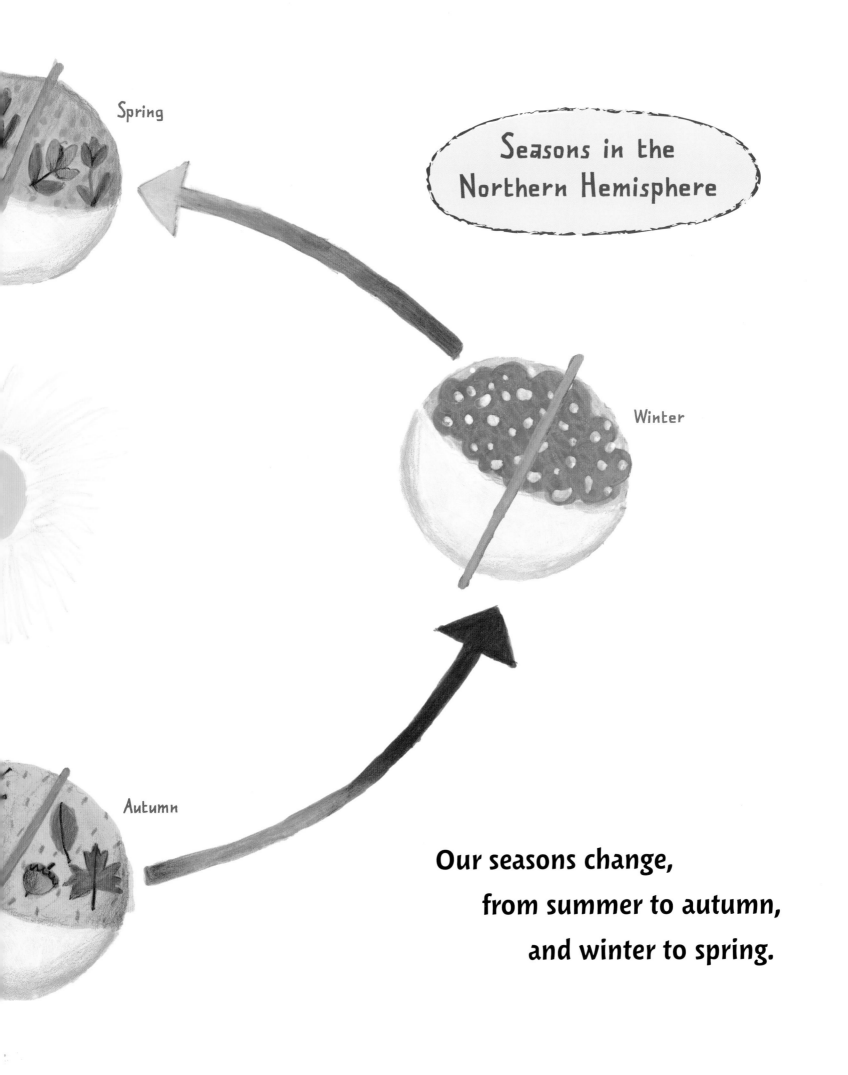

Spring

Winter

Autumn

Our seasons change,
from summer to autumn,
and winter to spring.

When the earth's top side
leans away from the sun

there is winter above the equator,
and summer below.

In winter the days get shorter and the nights are longer.

By spring the days get filled with sunlight.

We spin and we circle,
rotate and revolve,
but we don't fall off
(gravity holds us to the earth).

Gently. Slowly.
Around and around.
We hold out our arms
as we glide through the universe.

We fly through space
as night becomes day,
summer becomes winter,
and years go by.

THE EARTH

 The earth is like a ball,
it is a SPHERE.

 There is an imaginary line around
the center of the earth, the EQUATOR.

 The earth spins like a top.
It ROTATES around an imaginary line that
goes from top to bottom, the earth's AXIS.

 The earth REVOLVES around the sun
in a big oval ORBIT.

 There are imaginary points on the earth's top and
bottom, the NORTH POLE and the SOUTH POLE.

 GRAVITY is the force that holds us to the earth.